PROOF
YOU CAN'T IGNORE
THE MINI BOOK OF EVIDENCE FOR GOD, JESUS & THE BIBLE

GRANT GARWOOD

PROOF YOU CAN'T IGNORE, LLC

Proof You Can't Ignore
The Mini Book of Evidence for God, Jesus & the Bible

Published by
Proof You Can't Ignore, LLC
Towanda, Kansas

Copyright © 2025 Grant Garwood

ISBNs
Print: 979-8-9928063-0-4
Ebook: 979-8-9928063-1-1

Subjects:
REL067030 **RELIGION** / Christian Theology / Apologetics
REL030000 **RELIGION** / Christian Ministry / Evangelism
REL023000 **RELIGION** / Christian Ministry / Discipleship

All Scripture quotations, unless otherwise indicated, are taken from The Ryrie Study Bible, New International Version. Copyright © 1986, 1994 by The Moody Bible Institute by special arrangement with Zondervan Publishing House.

Any Internet addresses (websites, blogs, etc.) in this book are offered as a resource. They are not intended in any way to be or imply an endorsement by the publisher, nor does the publisher vouch for the content of these sites for the life of this book.

Printed in the United States

❀ Created with Vellum

CONTENTS

WHAT'S LIFE ALL ABOUT?

Several years ago, I found myself pondering questions that face all of us at some point in our lives. I grew up in a Christian home and adopted those beliefs at an early age. As an adult, however, I encountered a season where I wanted to be certain that what I had been taught and believed was trustworthy. Was what I counted as *absolute* truth *actually* true? I thought through the meaning of my life and about what really happens when someone dies. I realized that many of these answers hinged on whether or not the Bible was true. I needed to know if what the Bible said could be trusted and if it was something I could rely on to answer these crucial questions. This ultimately led me on a years-long intellectual journey to find the truth. This journey began not because I didn't believe the Bible but because I wanted to know if what I believed was reality.

What about you? Maybe you believe there is no God at all. Maybe you think there is a higher power but that the God of the Bible isn't a true picture of the creator. Maybe you think Jesus existed but that he was nothing more than a moral teacher or a social justice advocate. Whatever it is that we believe, wouldn't it be intellectually dishonest to continue with that belief if there was greater evidence to the contrary? That was the inquiry that began my quest to find where the evidence pointed and my commitment to believing whatever it was that the truth pointed me toward.

Though our starting points may be different, we both have the obligation to see where the evidence leads. We will either discover that the evidence proves our original belief (and maybe even what we *hope* to be true), or we will find that the evidence steers us away from the conclusion with which we first began. In either case, I believe our outcome will be the same if we are truly seeking objective truth. The evidence *will* lead us to a verdict. So, what does the evidence say? What does it mean? And what do we do with the truth we arrive at?

To arrive at an accurate verdict on truth, we must address and answer three main issues. First, does God exist? Second, is the Bible a trustworthy and reliable document? And third, if the Bible is reliable, what does it say about its central figure, Jesus, his claims to be God, and his followers' claims about his resurrection from the grave? If we can answer these questions beyond a "reasonable doubt," the pathway to truth is just around the corner.

In the following pages, I will attempt to lay out reasonable arguments for each question by using modern science, non-Biblical literature, archaeology, and the Bible. To be clear, this is not a comprehensive analysis of all areas of Christian apologetics but rather a "scratch the surface" overview of what I find to be some of the most reasonable and compelling evidence to date. Because this is more limited in scope, you will be responsible for doing further research on your own. Fact-check my work and investigate these claims for yourself. For a more detailed look into each question, you will find a list of additional resources at the end of this book.

Let's dive into the evidence.

1

DOES GOD EXIST?

Although there are many arguments for the existence of God, four lines of evidence stand out to me as being the most persuasive. Each argument is quite remarkable on its own, but when added together, they create a compelling case for the existence of an intelligent creator, whom I consider to be the God of the Bible.

In this chapter, we will explore the evidence of the uncaused first cause, fine-tuned universe, DNA by design, and objective morality. Perhaps by the end of this chapter, you may be persuaded to agree with former atheist Lee Strobel after he set out to disprove Christianity. He said, "To continue in atheism, I would need to believe that nothing produces everything, non-life produces life, randomness produces fine-tuning, chaos produces information, unconsciousness produces consciousness, and non-reason produces reason. I simply didn't have that much faith."[1]

THE UNCAUSED FIRST CAUSE
(THE COSMOLOGICAL ARGUMENT)

The first line of evidence to explore is the uncaused first cause, more formally known as the cosmological argument. Before we dig in, I want to say that we have jumped into the deep end. The cosmological argument is perhaps the most complex of the evidence I'll be presenting. If it seems overwhelming, move on to other evidence.

This cosmological argument seeks to define how the universe came into being. The uncaused first cause essentially asserts that anything that begins to exist has a cause. The best evidence seems to show that the universe *did* begin to exist. Therefore, the universe as we know it must have a cause. This cause must be uncaused and eternal. What is uncaused and eternal? The God of the Bible.

We packed a handful of claims into that previous paragraph, so now, let's unpack the evidence. Apologists Norman Geisler and Frank Turek have created an understandable and straight-forward outline for the cosmological argument through the acronym SURGE:

S – Second law of thermodynamics
U– Universe
R– Radiation afterglow
G– Great galaxy seeds
E– Einstein's theory of general relativity

The **S** stands for the second law of thermodynamics. Before we move into the second law, however, it's vitally important to know that the first law of thermodynamics states that the universe appears to have a certain amount of energy available to use. The second law of thermodynamics states that the universe is running *out* of this available energy. Geisler and Turek use a flashlight to illustrate this law. If you have a battery (finite amount of energy) in your flashlight and leave it on (consuming energy) for an extended time, the battery will eventually run out of energy and die. So, in essence, the second law of thermodynamics, among other things, says that the universe will one day run out of energy. If we will one day run out of energy, there is no possibility of our universe being eternal. As such, we must have had a beginning.[2]

The **U** stands for universe. Through the use of his telescope, Edwin Hubble was able to confirm that the universe is expanding. If the universe is expanding, how is it possibly eternal? If we extrapolate further, we can understand that if the universe is currently expanding, *reversing* history would take us back to a beginning, down to a small and finite universe. What was before the beginning? Absolutely nothing. If there was no space, no time, and no matter on which this universe could come into being, it implicitly means that something *outside* of space, time, and matter was the uncaused first cause. Scientists refer to the something out of nothing explosion as the big bang theory. Ironically, at that time, cosmologist Sir Fred Hoyle coined the phrase to mock the idea, as many atheists and agnostics were hesitant to acknowledge any kind of beginning as it would naturally point to a creator. During Q&A dialogues across the nation, Turek often says, "Oh I know there was a big bang, I just know what caused it and you don't!" If you're being intellectually honest, is it more reasonable to believe that something came from nothing and by nothing or that there was indeed an uncaused first cause?[3]

The **R** in SURGE stands for the radiation afterglow from the so-called big bang. In 1965, Arno Penzias and Robert Wilson accidentally discovered an unknown radiation on their antenna at Bell Labs in New Jersey. After more thorough investigation, they realized they had found the afterglow from what they believed to be the original cause of the universe. They received a Nobel Prize in physics in 1978 for their discovery. So, what exactly is this radiation? Formally known as background cosmic radiation, scientists believe this radiation is both light and heat from the start of the universe. Because of the expanding universe we've already mentioned, we cannot see the light because its wavelengths have been so dramatically stretched. The heat, however, can still be identified. This is one more piece of evidence for a universe start date.[4]

G stands for great galaxy seeds. If you don't have your thinking cap on yet, go ahead and put it on because you'll need it for this one. As scientists continued to study the big bang, they believed they would also find small variations in the temperature of radiation afterglow. After a NASA satellite mission returned in 1992, the findings were significant. Just as the scientists predicted, there were indeed variations of temperature in this radiation, but not only that; these variations showed that the massive explosion that caused the big bang was so precise that it allowed just enough matter to congregate to allow galaxy formation, but not enough to cause the universe to collapse immediately back on itself. Ultimately, these variations allowed matter to congregate, via gravitational pull, into galaxies, thus forming galaxy seeds. After the discovery, atheist and theoretical physicist Stephen Hawking said it was "the most important discovery of the century, if not of all time." Another piece of evidence for a universe start date.[5]

Finally, the **E** in SURGE stands for Einstein's theory of general relativity. This theory states that you cannot have only space or time or matter, they are interdependent on each other. Therefore, each of them must have come into existence at the same time. It should be noted that although this is indeed a "theory," it has been verified to five decimal places. On this theory, scientists began to explore letters **S** through **G** in our acronym.[6]

There we have it, **SURGE**. In totality, this evidence leads a reasonable person to believe that the universe indeed had a beginning and that the eternal or steady state theory, used as an argument against a creator, has scientific evidence to the contrary. Not only that, but it also has philosophical evidence to the contrary. Consider this. If the universe were eternal, how would we ever reach this point in time when it would take an infinite amount of time to reach the present from an eternal past? If the past is infinite, the present becomes unreachable. This is a nonsensical position.

So, what does this tell us? It tells us that anything that begins to exist has a cause, that the universe began to exist, therefore, the universe must have a cause. Because there was nothing in existence at some point (no space, no time, and no material), this "cause" must be spaceless, timeless, and immaterial. Astrophysicist Hugh Ross says that this evidence for cosmology "determines that the cause of the universe is functionally equivalent to the God of the Bible, a being beyond the matter, energy, space, and time of the cosmos."[7]

A FINE-TUNED UNIVERSE (THE ANTHROPIC PRINCIPLE)

The second line of evidence for the existence of a God is a fine-tuned universe. I consider this the single most fascinating and powerful argument. The minute details and absolute preciseness of our earth and entire universe are hard to fathom. It's impressive enough that one of the most well-known atheists of our day, the late Christopher Hitchens, who didn't give an inch for the possibility of a God, stated this when asked for the best argument from his Christian apologist counterparts. "The fine-tuning, that one degree, well, one degree, one hair [of difference] ... even though it doesn't prove design, doesn't prove a designer ... You have to spend time thinking about it, working on it. It's not a trivial [argument]. We all say that."[8] Even Richard Dawkins, an atheist as equally well known as Hitchens, said in a recent 2023 discussion with Francis Collins, the Former Head of the Genome Project and Science Advisor to the US President, that "If somebody was going to convince me of a need for a God, it would be there," referring to the fine-tuned argument.[9] So, what are some examples of this fine-tuning? Let's take a look.

Size of the Earth – If our Earth were slightly smaller, the reduced magnetic pull would not be powerful enough to protect us from the extreme amounts of electrons, protons, and alpha rays that come from our sun. The size of our Earth has just the right magnetosphere to protect us from these elements. If the Earth were slightly *larger*, the increased gravity would not allow methane or carbon dioxide to escape the atmosphere, making it impossible to breathe. Additionally, a similar life-inhibiting cause and effect would occur if our moon were slightly larger or smaller as well.[10]

Earth's location in the universe – If our solar system, which is situated just inside the Milky Way galaxy, were any closer to the center, the radiation from the stars near the center of the galaxy would be so significant that it would prohibit life. So not only is our Earth in the exact right place in our solar system for life to thrive, but also our solar system is in precisely the right place within our galaxy.[11]

Fundamental forces – If the strong nuclear force that holds protons and neutrons together were 0.3 percent stronger, only hydrogen could exist in our universe, and life would not be possible. If the electromagnetic force that allows electrons to orbit their nuclei appropriately were too great or too weak, the crucial elements needed for life on Earth would not exist. Furthermore, these two forces must maintain the exact ratio between each other. Paul Davis, an agnostic physicist, has calculated that if this ratio were off by one part in 10^{16}, life would not exist.[12]

Earth's oxygen levels – Our Earth currently has an oxygen level of 21 percent. If this level were slightly higher, fires would erupt at random. If this level were slightly lower, humans and animals would suffocate.[13]

Earth's carbon dioxide levels – Our Earth currently has a carbon dioxide level of 0.04 percent. If this level were slightly higher, our atmosphere would trap too much heat, and we would shrivel up. If this level were slightly lower, plants could not go through their required photosynthesis, and we would eventually suffocate.[14]

Gravitational pull – We rely on gravity and if the universe's gravitational force were changed by only 0.00000000000000000000000000000000000001 percent, the sun would not exist, which we know would make life impossible here on Earth.[15]

Planets' gravitational field – Jupiter, Saturn, Uranus, and Neptune are all precisely the right size and in the perfect location in relation to Earth. These gas giants keep the Earth from being pummeled by asteroids and contain just the right gravitational pull to allow for the crucial orbit of Earth.[16]

Earth's tilt – If the Earth did not perfectly maintain its 23.5-degree tilt, temperatures would become too extreme for life to exist.[17]

Universe density and expansion rate – In the words of atheist Stephen Hawking, "If the overall density of the universe were changed by even .0000000000001 percent, no stars or galaxies could be formed. If the rate of expansion one second after the big bang had been smaller by even one part in a hundred thousand million million, the universe would have re-collapsed before it reached its present size."[18]

Cosmological constant – According to Nobel Prize winner and atheist, Steven Weinberg, the energy density of the universe is so finely tuned that if this were off by one part in the 10^{120}, life would not exist. Just how much is 10^{120} you say? Unfathomable. For reference, the number of atoms in the entire known universe is estimated to be 10^{80}.[19]

Although I've mentioned just a few here, more than 140 finely tuned constants must be in place for even the most basic life forms to exist. If one looks at the fine-tuning evidence needed to support advanced life, this number balloons to over 1,300. Some of these examples are incredible and difficult for our human brains to comprehend, but what does all this mean, and why does it matter? Fred Hoyle, the famous astrophysicist, was a staunch atheist throughout his career. Still, when he began to discover the enormous amount of evidence building for the fine-tuned universe argument as modern science began to progress, his views began to change. In his book, *The Universe: Past and Present Reflections*, he says, "If one proceeds directly and straight-forwardly in this matter without being deflected by a fear of incurring the wrath of scientific opinion, one arrives at the conclusion that biomaterials with their amazing measure of order must be the outcome of intelligent design. No other possibility I have been able to think of in pondering this issue over quite a long time seems to me to have anything like as high a possibility of being true."[20] Although it doesn't appear that Hoyle believed in the God of the Bible as I do, he certainly held to the belief of an intelligent designer, which speaks volumes.

DNA BY DESIGN (THE TELEOLOGICAL ARGUMENT)

Keeping pace with the jaw-dropping fine-tuned universe argument, the DNA by design argument is equally astonishing but occurs in the world of biology. The evidence of an intelligent being serving as the creator of biological life is far more reasonable than the idea that random processes have perfected a genetic code more than three billion letters long.[21]

Let's take a trip down memory lane to when we first encountered the theory of how life began in our elementary school science textbooks. These textbooks told us that life begins through matter randomly evolving into a single cell, essentially saying that we get life from non-life. The books said there were enough random coincidences of non-living material that finally, one moment, millions of years into the existence of the universe, the perfect concoctions collided with each other, and formed life, giving us our first living cell. Even though this has never been observed or recreated with all the tools at our disposal or with the intelligent minds of scientists throughout history, this has somehow become the default assumption to which scientists have clung. Mathematician John Lennox suggests this line of thinking is an untenable position. He writes, "A world in which clever mathematical laws all by themselves bring the universe and life into existence is pure (science) fiction. Theories and laws do not bring matter or energy into existence or anything else. The view that they nevertheless somehow have that capacity seems a rather desperate refuge."[22]

Back to DNA. To lay the foundation of the DNA by design argument, it is helpful to understand the role that DNA plays in the creation of biological systems. In 1953, James Watson and Francis Crick were working in their usual lab at Cavendish Laboratory at the University of Cambridge when they discovered the famous double helix structure, known as deoxyribonucleic acid, or DNA for short. This groundbreaking discovery eventually led to them receiving the Nobel Prize in 1962. The study of molecular biology was never the same.

But why is DNA so important? Although Watson and Crick did not believe in an intelligent designer themselves, their discovery would serve as the foundation for one of the greatest arguments *for* an intelligent designer. Much like digital code on a computer that instructs the computer to perform a specific function, DNA is a biological code. The rungs of the DNA "ladder" are represented by the letters A, T, C, and G (the code). This code spells out a unique message like a genetic alphabet, if you will, creating the instructions for the basic building blocks of all living organisms. Said differently, DNA carries the genetic information necessary for the development, function, and reproduction of all living organisms.

The function and capability of DNA are extremely complex, but at an elementary level, DNA provides precise instructions to amino acids, which in turn provide their own specific instructions to create proteins. Each protein produced from this process provides a different but crucial function to the cell in which it's contained. Much like a tool in a toolbox, each protein serves a specific purpose and has an important job function within the cell. For example, the hemoglobin protein is responsible for carrying oxygen throughout our bodies. Defense proteins, known as antibodies, help fight off infection and diseases. Certain enzyme proteins help break down food for our bodies to absorb and be used as fuel. More than 100,000 proteins perform unique but vital functions in the cells of the human body. For context, just how many cells are there in the human body? Trillions.

So, how much of this genetic code is required for even the most basic life forms? Atheist Richard Dawkins says, "There is enough storage capacity in the DNA of a single lily seed or a single salamander sperm to store the Encyclopedia Britannica sixty times over. Some species of the unjustly called 'primitive' amoebas have as much information in their DNA as 1,000 Encyclopedia Britannicas."[23] Do you see how unlikely it is for this amount of densely packed information to exist without the input of an intelligent mind? This doesn't just highlight the *amount* of information stored in a single-celled amoeba (which would be incredible enough by itself) but also shows how precisely this information is *ordered*. Do you see the difference? Encyclopedias contain a massive number of words, but without the words being in a particular order, none of them would have any meaning. Think about the game of Scrabble. If you pour out the box of letters onto the table, are the words ever arranged in such a way that says, "Michael Jordan was the greatest" or "The sky is blue?" Of course not. An intelligent mind is needed to create these messages.

In his book *Signature in the Cell*, geophysicist Stephen Meyer gives us some perspective on the probability of a single functional protein being created by mere chance alone in a prebiotic environment. "With odds standing at one chance in 10,164 of finding a functional protein among the possible 150 amino-acid compounds, the probability is 84 orders of magnitude (or powers of ten) smaller than the probability of finding the marked particle in the whole universe. Another way to say that is the probability of finding a functional protein by chance alone is a trillion, trillion, trillion, trillion, trillion, trillion, trillion times smaller than the odds of finding a single specified particle among all the particles in the universe."[24] The idea that mindless processes throughout time led to the precise construction of DNA seems far more unreasonable to me than the idea of a creator God with an intelligent mind.

OBJECTIVE MORALITY (THE AXIOLOGICAL ARGUMENT)

Shifting gears from using modern science to make the case for the existence of God, let's turn our focus to one of the oldest and most well-known arguments in history: objective morality. This argument points out that morality is not simply *subjective* or based solely on personal taste or dislike. Rather, it's based on an *objective* morality that has been written on our hearts by a moral lawgiver. This standard of rightness or moral law is the very nature of the God of the Bible.

As much as some hate to admit it, we all have a sense of what is right and what is wrong. Of course, we don't always *do* what is right, but we do indeed *know* what is right. This standard of morality doesn't change with culture, location, or time period but transcends humanity. In his book *I Don't Have Enough Faith to Be an Atheist,* apologist Frank Turek provides an appropriate example of this transcendent law with the following story. At the conclusion of World War II, the Allied countries held the famous Nuremberg Trials. The goal of these trials was to seek justice against the Nazi war criminals for their crimes against humanity. If there were no international "code of conduct" for human rights, then the Allied countries would have no grounds to punish the Nazis appropriately. As Turek says, "We couldn't have said that the Nazis were absolutely wrong unless we knew what was absolutely right. But we do know they were absolutely wrong, so the Moral Law must exist."[25]

Now, if you're reading this and think, "I don't need God to know what's right and wrong. Hitler and Nazi Germany were outliers and didn't seek the highest good of others." I would then ask by what standard? How do you know what is inherently good and what is inherently bad without having a standard of morality outside of humanity? Because if there is no objective standard with which to compare, then all we have are our own opinions of morality and Hitler's actions would be completely justified. Why? Well, in Hitler's opinion, the Jews were an inferior race and allowing them to live was allowing them to disgrace humanity.

What's more, if life randomly began from a perfect concoction of primordial soup (as many of our science textbooks say), then there is no moral standard at all. In this scenario, all our thoughts and decisions are merely chemical reactions in our brains. And if that's the case, then none of us has a responsibility to refrain from murder or stealing. After all, why should we be held accountable for random chemical reactions in our brains that are out of our control? By taking this position, one is forced to admit that Hitler was not morally wrong but instead just had an opinion that was different from the general population.

Now, if you're reading this and still believe there is no absolute standard of morality and it's all subjective, let's consider an example for the moral relativist.

Imagine your son is playing in his final football game in high school. It's the last play of the state championship game, and his team is winning by three points. In a last-ditch effort to win the game, the opposing team throws a Hail Mary pass to their receiver in the end zone. The receiver catches the ball, and the referee signals a touchdown. It's clear to everyone watching, however, that the receiver was nearly a yard out of bounds when he caught the ball, making it an incomplete pass, and your son's team the new state champions. But after huddling together, the lead referee makes the official announcement. "The receiver was out of bounds when the ball was caught, but due to the incredible design and color of their uniforms, the ruling on the field is a touchdown." Your team and fans are irate at the thought of losing the state championship on a call that the referees *know* is wrong!

The idea is this: If you think there is no objective morality, have someone treat you unfairly and see how you respond. How did you react the last time someone cut in line at the Black Friday holiday sale or when your underperforming colleague received a year-end bonus and you didn't? How you respond to unfairness speaks volumes about your position on morality. In the end, I believe it is more logical to conclude that there is a transcendent moral law that is written on our hearts and guides our conscience. If there is indeed an objective moral law, by necessity, there must be a moral lawgiver.

CONCLUSION

Although we only briefly touched on each of the four arguments, they are each compelling proof that there is indeed a God. I believe this evidence indicates this is a personal God who created the universe from nothing, precisely orchestrated its arrangement to an unfathomable exactness, designed biological life with extraordinary detail and order, and wrote a transcendent standard of rightness on the hearts and minds of every human being.

2

IS THE BIBLE RELIABLE?

In 1974, *Time Magazine* published an article regarding the reliability of the Bible. It concluded by saying, "After more than two centuries of facing the heaviest guns that could be brought to bear, the Bible has survived. ... The Scriptures seem more acceptable now than they did when the rationalists began their attack."[1] Is this true? Is this book historically reliable? How can we be sure the original writers didn't fashion their own narrative or that the subject matter hasn't been changed over the course of time? At first glance, it may seem reasonable to assume that such an old book could easily be altered, and the content we have today is the best guess of what was originally written. Has it?

Let's provide some helpful context before we dive into our analysis of this book. The Bible is divided between the Old Testament (before Jesus' birth) and the New Testament (after Jesus' birth). It was written by nearly forty different authors over a 2,500-year period. It's recorded in three languages, with the Old Testament written primarily in Hebrew and the New

Testament written primarily in Greek, with a few passages in Aramaic. Written across three different continents, its geographic footprint is vast. In the words of apologist Alex McFarland, "The evidence of history, consistency, testimony, and fulfillment all point toward a book that is indestructible and life-changing today."[2]

Although we could provide hundreds of examples to point to the reliability of the Bible, our focus will be a narrow selection of the most compelling evidence to date. We will see examples of non-Christian writings and archaeology corroborating the Scriptures, the historical eyewitness testimony within the Bible, and why the Old Testament prophecies play a significant role in its trustworthiness. I will attempt to show that its contents do not coincide with fairy tale or legend. The Bible contains real people, real places, and real events, all working in unison to show its authenticity.

NON-CHRISTIAN WRITINGS

When considering the historical reliability of ancient texts, historians use a set of criteria to determine the accuracy of a specific writing. When applying this set of rules to the Bible itself, it shows a high level of accuracy. (I will expand more on this later.) But what about sources outside of the Bible? Do we have writings from ancient historians who were not Christians but still corroborate what it says?

You may be surprised to learn that more than sixty outside sources corroborate various references in the Bible. Ten known non-Christian writers mention Jesus specifically. Although I encourage you to research each one, below are four independent literary sources that corroborate the Bible.

Tacitus

Cornelius Tacitus was an ancient Roman historian who wrote the *Annals* and the *Histories*. He lived from approximately AD 56–AD 120. In the *Annals of Tacitus*, he records that Nero, the Roman emperor at that time, blamed the Christians for a fire that broke out in Rome. In the next sentence, he also mentions the Emperor Tiberius Caesar and Pontius Pilate. Matthew 27 tells us that Pontius Pilate was the procurator (governor) of Judea at the time of Jesus' crucifixion and presided over his death.

> *"Early in the morning, all the chief priests and the elders of the people came to the decision to put Jesus to death. They bound him, led him away and handed him over to Pilate, the governor."*
> (Matthew 27:1–2)

> *"Consequently, to get rid of the report, Nero fastened the guilt and inflicted the most exquisite tortures on a class hated for their abominations, called Christians by the populace. Christus, from whom the name had its origin, suffered the extreme penalty during the reign of Tiberius at the hands of one of our procurators, Pontius Pilatus, and a most mischievous superstition, thus checked for the moment, again broke out not only in Judaea, the first source of the evil, but even in Rome, where all things hideous and shameful from every part of the world find their centre and become popular. Accordingly, an arrest was first made of all who pleaded guilty; then, upon their information, an*

immense multitude was convicted, not so much of the crime of firing the city, as of a hatred against mankind. Mockery of every sort was added to their deaths. Covered with the skins of beasts, they were torn by dogs and perished, or were nailed to crosses, or were doomed to the flames and burnt, to serve as a nightly illumination, when daylight had expired."[3]

Thallus (Quoted by Julius Africanus)

Although not as much is known about Thallus himself because most of his works have been lost, we know he was a Samaritan historian who wrote extensively about the history of the Mediterranean world. We do, however, have several fragments of his writings and quotes documented by other ancient historians in the early AD 50s. Perhaps the most well-known quote of Thallus was detailed by Sextus Julius Africanus as Thallus attempted to explain away the darkness that overtook the land on the day Jesus died as an ironic coincidence. As seen below, however, Africanus disagreed with Thallus' assumption. We know from the book of Matthew that for approximately three hours leading up to Jesus' final breath, from 12:00 p.m. to 3:00 p.m., darkness covered the land. In the ancient Jewish tradition, 12:00 p.m. was the sixth hour of the day. (It should be noted that Africanus also similarly quoted Phlegon, another secular historian.)

"From the sixth hour until the ninth hour darkness came over all the land." (Matthew 27:45)

"On the whole world there pressed a most fearful darkness; and the rocks were rent by an earth-

quake, and many places in Judea and other districts were thrown down. This darkness Thallus, in the third book of his History, calls, as appears to me without reason, an eclipse of the sun."[4]

"Phlegon records that in the time of Tiberius Caesar, at full moon, there was a full eclipse of the sun from the sixth hour to the ninth."[5]

Suetonius

Gaius Suetonius Tranquillus was another ancient Roman historian who wrote several works, including twelve biographies of Roman emperors, including Julius Caesar, Domitian, Tiberius, Nero, and Claudius. Suetonius lived from approximately AD 69–AD 122. Although there appears to be more than one reference in his writings that corroborates the Bible, the most well-known is recorded in his work, *The Life of Claudius*. In this book, he confirms what is mentioned in Acts 18, where Luke writes that Claudius ordered all the Jews to leave Rome.

"There he [Apostle Paul] met a Jew named Aquila, a native of Pontus, who had recently come from Italy with his wife Priscilla, because Claudius had ordered all the Jews to leave Rome." (Acts 18:2)

"As the Jews were making constant disturbances at the instigation of Chrestus, he (Claudius) expelled them from Rome."[6] (Life of Claudius 25.4)

Josephus

Flavius Josephus was a military commander whom many consider the most famous Jewish historian. He lived from approximately AD 37–AD 100 and was tasked with recording Jewish history. He wrote *The Jewish War, Antiquities of the Jews, Against Apion,* and later, his autobiography. In the *Antiquities of the Jews,* Josephus gives a brief life story of a "wise man" named Jesus.

> "At this time there was a wise man who was called Jesus. His conduct was good, and [he] was known to be virtuous. And many people from among the Jews and the other nations became his disciples. Pilate condemned him to be crucified and to die. And those who had become his disciples did not abandon his discipleship. They reported that he had appeared to them three days after his crucifixion and that he was alive; accordingly, he was perhaps the Messiah concerning whom the prophets have recounted wonders."[7] (Antiquities of the Jews 18:3)

Later in the *Antiquities of the Jews,* he also confirms a passage in Matthew 14 that outlines the imprisonment and death of John the Baptist, a key figure during the early stages of Jesus' ministry.

> "The king [Herod] was distressed, but because of his oaths and his dinner guests, he ordered that her request be granted and had John beheaded in the prison. His head was brought in on a platter and given to the girl, who carried it to her mother." (Matthew 14:9–11)

> "Now, some of the Jews thought that the destruction

of Herod's army came from God, and very justly,
as a punishment of what he did against John, who
was called the Baptist; for Herod slew him, who
was a good man, and commanded the Jews to exer-
cise virtue, both as to righteousness towards one
another and piety towards God, and so to come to
baptism."[8] (Antiquities of the Jews 18:5)

BIBLICAL ARCHAEOLOGY

After examining a handful of independent historical
writings from non-Christians that appear to substan-
tiate the Bible, we will shift our focus to historical
artifacts that do likewise. For centuries, skeptics
would point to different passages in the Bible and
assume that because there was no concrete evidence
available, there was no reason to believe it was true.
With continued excavation in the regions where the
Israelites were known to live and where Jesus spent
much of his time, archaeologists are finding more
artifacts that corroborate both Old and New
Testament Scriptures. Like the non-Christian writings, we could point to many artifacts, but due to the
amount of context needed to build the case, readers
will need to do additional research on their own.

The Pilate Stone and the Pontius Pilate Ring

As we saw in the previous section from the historian
Tacitus, Pontius Pilate was a Roman governor over
Judea who served under Emperor Tiberius Caesar
from AD 26–AD 36. Pilate oversaw Jesus' trial and
ultimately succumbed to the Jews' demand to send
Jesus to the cross. In 1961, an Italian archaeologist
named Dr. Antonio Frova discovered the Pilate stone
while excavating in Caesarea, located in northern

Israel. It was embedded in stone steps leading to Caesarea's amphitheater. Although only a fragment was found, it says,

> To the Divine August [this] Tiberieum
> ... Pontius Pilate
> ... prefect of Judea
> ... has dedicated [this]

We know from other historical documents that Tiberius reigned from AD 14–AD 37, and, as mentioned above, Pontius Pilate was the governor serving under him from AD 26–AD 36. This lines up with the Biblical timeline of Jesus' death on the cross, which most Biblical scholars believe took place in either AD 30 or AD 33.[9]

Additionally, in 1969, a copper and alloy ring was discovered at Herodium, an ancient fortress of Herod the Great. In late 2018, when the ring was thoroughly cleaned and examined using improved technology, an inscription was discovered that read, "Pilato," which is Greek for Pontius Pilate.[10]

House of David Stele (Tel Dan Stele)

In the Old Testament book of 1 Samuel, we read about David's defeat of Goliath with only a sling and a smooth stone. David eventually became the King of Israel and served as king until he died at age seventy. In 1993, the first of three stone fragments were found in Tel Dan in northern Israel. This stone contained an inscription written to celebrate the victory of an Aram king over Israel and Judea. Part of the inscription says, "I killed Jehoram son of [Ahab] King of Israel... And I slew the king of the House of

David." Although the name of that king is not included on the fragment, we know it was written in Aramaic by an Aramaic king. It is likely the king was Hazael of Damascus, who would have been king around this time and is also mentioned in the Old Testament book of 2 Kings. This inscription does not mention King David himself, but it references the House of David, which is mentioned many times throughout the Bible and refers to King David specifically.[11]

The Caiaphas Ossuary

We know from the Gospel accounts that Caiaphas was a Jewish high priest who was influential among the Jewish leaders in sending Jesus to the cross. In 1990, an ornate limestone box, called an ossuary, was found in Jerusalem. What's an ossuary? From about 20 BC to AD 70, important people in the Jewish culture were buried and then later had their bones dug up and placed in an ossuary. This particular ossuary is significant because on its side, it identifies the contents as the bones of Caiaphas. Inside the box are the remains of a sixty-year-old man and his family.[12]

Papyrus Brooklyn

In the Old Testament book of Exodus, we read about the Israelites being enslaved by an Egyptian Pharaoh. In approximately 1446 BC, God commanded Moses to go to the Pharaoh and tell him to let the Israelite people go, freeing them from their bondage. Pharaoh was too proud to release his army of slaves and said no, which led to God sending ten plagues to Egypt. By the end of the tenth plague, which involved the

Pharaoh's own son dying, he conceded and allowed the Israelites to leave Egypt.

The mass exodus out of Egypt played a large role in the Israelites' history, so it was significant when the Papyrus Brooklyn was found in southern Egypt. The Papyrus Brooklyn is an Egyptian papyrus from around 1600 BC. It was found in southern Egypt and contains a list of household slaves. When the names were analyzed, approximately thirty-seven were Semitic (Israelite/Hebrew) names replaced with new Egyptian names. Further, nine of those names were biblical Hebrew names. For example, the name Shiphrah is on this list. We know from Exodus 1:15 that this is the name of one of the Hebrew midwives Pharaoh spoke to when commanding these midwives to kill all Hebrew baby boys but allow the baby girls to live. With this papyrus, we now have concrete evidence that people with Hebrew names (Israelites) lived in Egypt just prior to the Exodus. And not only that, but we also have an Egyptian document showing these individuals were slaves.[13]

The Dead Sea Scrolls

Although the previous artifacts mentioned here have all been significant in bolstering the reliability of the Bible, the Dead Sea Scrolls may be the greatest discovery of them all. In 1947, a young shepherd boy was tending to his flock of goats in Qumran, just east of Jerusalem. Apparently one goat wandered off into the cliffs and the twelve-year-old boy followed suit. As he searched for the goat, he randomly threw a rock into one of the many deep caves overlooking the Dead Sea. He expected to hear one rock crashing against another, so when it sounded more like a crash of pottery, he was intrigued. The young boy crawled into the cave and discovered not one but hundreds of clay jars. This discovery, which led to searching other nearby caves, contained a collection of nearly a thousand scrolls in total. Due to the stable temperature and lack of wind in the caves, each scroll was astonishingly well preserved.

Now, the importance of this discovery is twofold. Before the shepherd boy stumbled upon these jars, the earliest manuscripts (scrolls) we had for the books of the Old Testament (written before Jesus' birth) were from around AD 900, or about 870 years after Jesus' death on the cross. As a result, many skeptics believed the predicted prophecies that Jesus fulfilled in the New Testament (written after Jesus' birth) were written after the fact and were, therefore, unreliable and unsubstantiated. The Dead Sea Scrolls blew a hole straight through that theory, as they are dated between 300 BC and AD 70. Not only does this mean that we now have manuscripts 1,200 years earlier than previously discovered, but we also are absolutely certain that these crucial Old Testament books, Isaiah and Psalms in particular, were written *before* Jesus was born. The idea that the fulfilled prophecies were invented only after Jesus died is no longer a logical position. (A list of these prophecies and their fulfillment is provided later in this chapter.)

News of the Dead Sea Scrolls rocked the world. Skeptics who heard the news began lining up to examine the texts. This was the opportunity they had been waiting for to compare manuscripts side-by-side over a two-thousand-year period. Surely this would show how drastically the scribes had changed the text to match their biased narrative. After nearly five decades of examining the manuscripts, the skeptics had nothing to celebrate. The accuracy of the writings was beyond what anyone imagined. The care the scribes took in copying the text over time delivered an extremely precise and accurate replication of these manuscripts throughout this 2,000-year history. (Additional information on the consistency of New Testament manuscripts follows in the next section.)[14]

MANUSCRIPT EVIDENCE

To continue examining the reliability of the Bible, we will sharpen our focus to the twenty-seven books of the New Testament and attempt to determine the following: Has the New Testament been changed over the course of 2,000 years? Was it written early enough to be reliable? Were there eyewitnesses? If so, were the eyewitnesses accurate? Were the eyewitnesses changed by what they witnessed? And were there prophecies fulfilled by Jesus that help confirm the reliability of the Bible?

Manuscript Volume and Dating

One of the most common objections to the reliability of the New Testament is its age. How can we be sure that these twenty-seven independent documents haven't been changed? Wouldn't it be easy for someone to obtain a copy, make revisions more conducive to the author's viewpoint, and then pass it along as a reliable text? At first glance, it's reasonable to assume this could have happened over the course of generations. So how can we be sure that it hasn't?

In ancient literature, scholars use two sets of criteria to determine the level of trustworthiness of any given work. The higher the number of manuscripts found and the earlier the manuscripts were written after the original, the higher the degree of reliability. So how does the New Testament stack up with other ancient literature on these two fronts? By volume, the New Testament has over 5,700 partial or complete written Greek manuscripts to date.[15] When including all other languages, that number balloons to over 20,000 and is still growing.[16] The next closest ancient work, the *Iliad* by Homer, is far behind with 643 total manuscripts. There is simply no other document from the ancient world with this level of manuscript support.

By date, New Testament manuscripts have been found as early as AD 117–AD 138[17], with some disputed manuscripts dated from AD 50–AD 70. (As a reminder, Jesus was crucified in the early AD 30s.) Because Roman Emperor Diocletian ordered that all manuscripts and churches be destroyed in AD 303, having any manuscripts this early is noteworthy. When compared to the next closest ancient literary work by date—also the *Iliad*—the first surviving copy is nearly 500 years after the original was written.[18] Even writings from Aristotle, Herodotus, Euripides, and Sophocles have a gap of 1,300–1,500 years between the original writings and the most recent copies.[19] Does anyone question the authenticity of these works? Former atheist Josh McDowell's mission to discredit the Bible ultimately led to his conversion to Christianity. He said, "After trying to shatter the historicity, validity, and authenticity of the Scriptures, I came to the conclusion that the Bible is historically trustworthy. I also discovered that if one discards the Bible as being unreliable, then one must discard almost immediately all literature of antiquity."[20]

Before we move on to the next section, it's helpful to address a common assertion often made when considering these manuscripts. The statement usually goes something like this: The Bible has been translated so many times over several thousand years that it's been lost in translation. Maybe it has. With the sheer number of manuscripts available, the issue of translation could be a serious matter. Let's take a closer look.

The primary languages of the Bible are Hebrew and Greek. So how were the manuscripts translated from one language to another? Was the Bible translated from Greek to Latin to French to Russian to Swahili to Arabic to Chinese and then finally to English, leading to theological erosion of the original meaning? This is not the case. When the Old Testament is rendered for us here in America, it's translated from the original Hebrew to English. Likewise, when the New Testament is translated, it's translated from the original Greek to English. This is a very common practice in literature and does not take away from the original meaning of the text. Having said this, if people are skeptical of these translations, they could learn the original languages themselves and join more than 20 million people across the globe who still use Hebrew and Greek today.

Manuscript Integrity

Now that we know there are a significant number of manuscripts and how early some of them were written, how do they compare to one another? Are there any differences in the text, or more specifically, variants that change the message or doctrine of the New Testament? This is often a topic where misconceptions run rampant, so we must address some common misunderstandings and provide the appropriate context for our analysis. In his book *Misquoting Jesus*, atheist Bart Ehrman points out that between 200,000–400,000 textual variants can be found throughout the known manuscripts.[21] To put this into perspective, there are only about 138,000 words in the entire New Testament! If one goes no further in this investigation, it may lead you to believe that the New Testament is so scattered with inconsistencies that all of it should be called into question. And with that level of skepticism of the text, why would anyone have reason to believe anything in this book is true?

As I've similarly stated in other sections, the area of textual criticism is one that someone should research further to understand the quantity and types of variants found in the text. But, to keep this relatively brief, let's examine a few important points.

First, I need to acknowledge that Ehrman is indeed correct when he says there are between 200,000–400,000 variants in the known New Testament manuscripts. But the real question we need to ask is, what kind of variants are we talking about? The vast majority are differences in the spelling of a word, inverse word order, substituted synonyms, and non-viable variants, essentially inconsequential material in which nearly all scholars agree. When you consider that most Greek manuscripts were written in capital letters with no word spacing and no punctuation, this is unsurprising.[22] For context, in English, this would be like writing "We walked around Washington DC singing Kumbaya, My Lord!" as

"WEWALKEDAROUNDWASHINGTONDCSING-INGKUMBAYAMYLORD." This is only nine words. Imagine writing this letter by letter for the 138,000 words in the New Testament!

There are, however, a few variants (less than 1 percent), such as the ending of the book of Mark and Jesus graciously confronting the woman caught in adultery in John 7 and 8, where scholars question their inclusion in the text.[23] Some manuscripts contain these passages, but many of the earliest ones do not. In many cases, the scribes would notate a clarification or indicate the question about a particular verse or passage in a footnote, much like we see in our Bibles today. These examples are among the most significant variants in the entire New Testament. As New Testament scholar Craig Blomberg concludes in his book *The Historical Reliability of the New Testament,* no variants affect a single doctrine of Christianity.[24] And even though Ehrman attempts to cast doubt on the Bible throughout *Misquoting Jesus*, he agrees with Blomberg, admitting that no essential doctrine of the Bible is affected by these variants.[25]

Original Writings

We have just explored the evidence for some of the oldest manuscripts found to date. But these are not the originals, only copies. So, when were the *original* New Testament books actually written? Although many scholars believe the majority of the New Testament was written by AD 100, some believe nearly all the books were written by at least AD 70, or approximately forty years after Jesus' death and resurrection. The main piece of evidence for this dating is the lack of mentioning the destruction of King Herod's temple in Jerusalem by the Romans in September of AD 70 after a Jewish rebellion in AD 66. (This also included the brutal murder of over one million Jews and over 100,000 more taken as slave laborers for the Roman empire.) For Jews at that time, the destruction of the temple would have been far more significant than the fall of the Twin Towers for Americans in 2001.

No New Testament book shows any indication of the temple being destroyed or the murder of a million Jews. It's also important to note that Jesus predicted the destruction of this temple in Matthew 24:1–3, which says, "Jesus left the temple and was walking away when his disciples came up to him to call his attention to its buildings. 'Do you see all these things?' Jesus asked. 'I tell you the truth, not one stone here will be left on another; every one will be thrown down.'" We know that in AD 70, the Emperor Titus destroyed the temple by accident when one of his men threw a burning stick into the temple during the chaos of battle. The burning of the temple ultimately led to the Romans tearing it down, brick by brick. New Testament writers would certainly have included the fulfillment of this prophecy if any of these books were written post-AD 70.

If most of the books were written before AD 100 or even AD 70, are there some that we can date closer to Jesus' time on earth? Cross-referencing content between the books in the New Testament and extra-Biblical resources, we can create a reasonable timeline of authorship. In the book of Acts, the author (Luke) indicates that Stephen and James (brother of John) have recently been martyred, but both Paul and James (brother of Jesus) were still living. Clement of

Rome records that Paul was executed by Nero no later than AD 68. The historian Josephus writes that James (brother of Jesus) was martyred in AD 62, providing strong evidence that the book of Acts was written by AD 62.[26] Furthermore, Paul authored the books (letters) of Romans, 1 Corinthians, 2 Corinthians, and Galatians, which are all dated between AD 48 and AD 60 by even the most skeptical New Testament scholars. And although some credit Matthew as being the first gospel recorded, there is also strong evidence that Mark is the earliest gospel, written anywhere between AD 45 and AD 50, followed by Luke between AD 50 and AD 53.[27] Atheist and originator of the "Death of God" movement, John A.T. Robinson, concluded in his book *Redating the New Testament* that all four gospels were written between AD 40 and AD 65.

Even though these are incredibly early writings from an ancient historical context, you still might be thinking, I can't remember what I had for breakfast this morning, let alone what I was doing twenty years ago! Many events written about in the Bible, however, were what are called "impact events," meaning they had an enormous impact or significance on the individual's life. Cold-case homicide detective and former atheist J. Warner Wallace talks about these impact events in his book *Cold-Case Christianity*. "When eyewitnesses encounter an event that is similarly unique, unrepeated, and powerful, they are far more likely to remember it and recall specific details accurately."[28] Do you remember where you were and what you were doing when you heard the news of the first plane that crashed into the World Trade Center on September 11, 2001? If you were in the motorcade directly behind John F. Kennedy when he was assassinated in 1963, do you think you would vividly recall those moments? These are impact events. Think about the disciples watching Jesus raise a dead child back to life, healing a man of leprosy, and giving sight to a blind man. These are events that had a significant emotional impact on the disciples, leading to detailed written accounts.

Although I cover this in greater detail as evidence for the resurrection of Jesus, it is vitally important to mention the tremendous value that the early Christian creeds play as a part of the earliest evidence for the claims of Jesus. Because nearly 90 percent of the people in the first century were illiterate, it was important to communicate the basic foundations of Jesus' teachings, death on the cross, burial, and resurrection in oral form so it could be passed from one person to another. You will see later that even the most skeptical New Testament scholars date the formation of these creeds to within three to five years after Jesus' death, with many of them dating the formation to within a few *months* after his death. More than forty creeds are included in the New Testament. This ultimately tells us that although it may have taken some time to record the New Testament books in writing, the sources and basis for these writings derived almost immediately after Jesus' death, burial, and resurrection. Remember, this is the first century AD with no email, no texting, and no formal mail route. This is a tight timeline that I believe is extremely difficult for one to discredit rationally.

Eyewitness Testimony and Martyrdom of Jesus' Followers

The Bible includes a significant amount of eyewitness testimony. In the New Testament, for example, the Gospels of Matthew, Mark, Luke, and John provide four corroborating but unique biographies of Jesus. Having one or two eyewitnesses in the court of law is significant, so having four biographies of Jesus in this detail in ancient literature is remarkable. Skeptics, however, often say that Jesus' followers were biased and, therefore, their testimony cannot be of any evidential value. But as apologist Frank Turek often says, people lie, cheat, and steal for the purposes of sex, money, or power. These early eyewitnesses didn't get any of these benefits but instead got the opposite. They were hated for what they believed, and many of them were killed as martyrs.

Although their martyrdom is not the main evidence to prove the trustworthiness of the Gospels, it stands out to me as one of the most significant. When you think of martyrdom, you might be thinking, people die for causes they believe in all the time, this proves absolutely nothing. I agree. There is a fundamental difference, however, with the martyrdom of Jesus' followers. How so? His followers watched Jesus perform miracles, saw him nailed to a cross and crucified, and then saw him resurrected three days later. After witnessing his resurrection, they were fundamentally transformed and began to share what they had seen boldly. Because of their boldness, many of them were martyred. But herein lies the contrast. *His followers were the only people who were in a position to know if what they saw was actually true.* Do you see the difference? Why would someone needlessly die for something they *know* is a lie? Consider putting yourself in the shoes of his followers. With nothing to gain, would you die for something you *know* is a lie?

Old Testament Prophecies Fulfilled

Prophecies or future predictions are another way to determine the reliability of the Bible. The prophecies found throughout the Old Testament are predictions written hundreds of years before the events described in the New Testament. Although the Bible contains hundreds of prophecies, we will narrow our focus to the fulfilled prophecies specifically detailing Jesus as the coming Messiah.

The following texts come from various books of the Old Testament written between 500 and 1,500 years before Jesus' birth. As you read through these, ask yourself, is there anyone in human history who satisfies these prophecies. Does this fit what the Gospel writers describe in Matthew, Mark, Luke, and John? Even if just a few of these were legitimately fulfilled, does this not carry a significant amount of weight? Let's take a look.

> *"He was despised and rejected by men..."* (Isaiah 53:3)

Jesus was rejected, particularly within his own Jewish culture at the time. Matthew 21:42, Mark 12:10, and Acts 4:11 all mention that Jesus was the stone (or cornerstone) which the builders rejected. These verses not only correspond to Isaiah 53:3 but also to Psalm 118:22. (As we expand on Isaiah 53, it is important to note that the Jewish interpretation of

Isaiah 42-53 at that time, commonly known as the Suffering Servant passage, was that these chapters were indeed predictive of the coming Messiah.)

"But he was pierced for our transgressions, he was crushed for our iniquities; the punishment that brought us peace was upon him, and by his wounds we are healed." (Isaiah 53:5)

Matthew 27:35 says that Jesus was crucified on the cross for our transgressions (sins). What's more, the practice of crucifixion (piercing with nails) had not yet been invented when Isaiah was written, adding to the significance of this prophecy.

"And I will pour out on the house of David and the inhabitants of Jerusalem a spirit of grace and supplication." (Zechariah 12:10a)

"The days are coming, declares the Lord, when I will raise up to David a righteous Branch, a King who will reign wisely and do what is just and right in the land. In his days Judah will be saved and Israel will live in safety. This is the name by which he will be called: The Lord Our Righteousness." (Jeremiah 23:5-6)

Both the Zechariah and Jeremiah passages indicate that the Messiah would come from the lineage of David. In chapter one of Matthew's Gospel, we see the detailed genealogy of the fourteen generations from Abraham to David, the fourteen generations from David to the exile to Babylon, and the fourteen generations from the exile to Jesus.

"They will look on me, the one they have pierced,

*and they will mourn for him as one who mourns
for an only child, and grieve bitterly for him as
one grieves for a firstborn son."* (Zechariah
12:10b)

John 19:34 says that one of the soldiers pierced Jesus'
side with a spear while he was still on the cross,
making sure he was dead before taking him down.
What's more, we know from the most well-known
verse in the Bible, John 3:16, that "God so loved the
world that he gave his one and only Son, that who-
ever believes in him shall not perish but have eternal
life."

*"He was oppressed and afflicted, yet he did not open
his mouth ..."* (Isaiah 53:7a)

Mark 15:4-5 says that Pontius Pilate asked Jesus to
respond to the accusations of the chief priests (religious leaders) before his crucifixion, but Jesus made
no reply.

"... he was led like a lamb to the slaughter ..."
(Isaiah 53:7b)

Mark 15 says that Jesus was led out of the city and
forced to carry his own cross to Golgotha, where he
was crucified.

*"For he was cut off from the land of the living; for
the transgression of my people he was stricken."*
(Isaiah 53:8b)

Matthew, Mark, Luke, and John all tell us that after
Jesus was condemned, he was beaten and put to
death (cut off).

> *"They have pierced my hands and my feet. I can*
> *count all my bones; people stare and gloat over me.*
> *They divide my garments among them and cast lots*
> *for my clothing."* (Psalm 22:16b–18)

> *"He protects all his bones, not one of them will be*
> *broken."* (Psalm 34:20)

Matthew, Mark, Luke, and John outline Jesus' crucifixion in detail. These books show the mocking and gloating of the people and the soldiers in charge of Jesus. Lots were indeed cast for his clothing, and although unusual for Roman crucifixion, his bones were not broken. Typically, when a person was crucified on a cross, they would use their legs to push their body up enough to allow themselves to breathe. Eventually, a Roman soldier would break the individual's legs so they could no longer catch another breath and die of asphyxiation. In Jesus' case, he died before his legs were broken. This was confirmed when a Roman soldier pierced his side while on the cross, spilling out blood and water. Today, we know this is pericardial effusion, a reaction of Jesus' body to the intense flogging that led to a buildup of fluid around the heart.

> *"The scepter will not depart from Judah, nor the*
> *ruler's staff from between his feet, until he comes to*
> *whom it belongs and the obedience of the nations is*
> *his."* (Genesis 49:10)

Although somewhat difficult to understand, this passage explains that the ceremonial staff carried by a king (scepter) will remain in the tribe of Judah until the true Messiah comes. Matthew 1:3 and Luke 3:30

both show that Jesus was a descendant of the tribe of Judah.

> "For a child will be born to us, a Son will be given to us; and the government will rest on His shoulders; and his name will be called Wonderful Counselor, Mighty God, Eternal Father, Prince of Peace. There will be no end to the increase of His government or of peace, on the throne of David and over his kingdom, to establish it and to uphold it with justice and righteousness from then on and forevermore." (Isaiah 9:6–7, NASB)

Luke 2 lays out the birth narrative of Jesus and the entire New Testament testifies to his divinity. And, again, he is a descendant of David.

> "But you, O Bethlehem Ephrathah, are only a small village among all the people of Judah. Yet a ruler of Israel, whose origins are in the distant past, will come from you on my behalf." (Micah 5:2)

Luke 2 says Jesus was born in Bethlehem, exactly as predicted by the prophet Micah nearly 700 years before his birth.

CONCLUSION

At the start of this chapter, we stated that our goal was to determine if the Bible is a historically reliable document. Throughout history, skeptics have claimed that the Bible is not historically accurate and is a collection of fairy tales and legends, or, at best, deceptively altered to suit the desired narrative of the writers.

After reading this short list of evidence, does the Bible seem like a collection of fanciful fairy tales or legends to you? Is there reasonable evidence to conclude that the eyewitness testimony and historical early recordings of the events are accurate? Or what about the fulfilled Old Testament prophecies and the martyrdom of Jesus' followers? Is it more reasonable to conclude that his followers had a motive to concoct one of the biggest lies in history, or did they boldly proclaim what they had seen and heard because they had, indeed, seen the miracles and witnessed his resurrection? Once again, I believe the evidence presented answers the question of the Bible's reliability beyond a reasonable doubt.

3
WHAT DOES THE BIBLE
SAY ABOUT JESUS?

Now that we have reasonable evidence to conclude that God *does* exist and the Bible *is* reliable, we can logically trust what the Bible says. With that in mind, we must assess what the Bible says about Jesus. We will do so by zeroing in on the New Testament. Much is said about Jesus' life and ministry in the final twenty-seven books of the Bible, but to provide a brief yet impactful line of evidence for the skeptic, we will narrow our focus to two key areas. First, we need to establish what the Bible says about Jesus' claims to be God. Did he *actually* claim to be God, or was he really just an ethical teacher who made cryptic comments to cause controversy and grow his following of people? Because if Jesus didn't really claim to be God, then the debate regarding his life, death, and resurrection is meaningless. But, if we can sufficiently and reasonably conclude that Jesus did claim this deity, we can perhaps address the most important issue of all: his alleged resurrection from the grave.

LIAR, LUNATIC, OR LORD?

To adequately establish our first objective, we will respond to the claim that Jesus was just an ethical teacher. This appears to be a noncommittal, "middle of the road" response from skeptics who see a mountain of evidence that the historical Jesus did exist but do not believe that Jesus is who he said he was. It appears to me that an honest study of the text will lead one to believe that Jesus was either a fraud, a madman, or Lord, with no middle ground on which to fall. A choice must be made. C.S. Lewis articulates this point much more eloquently than I do. In his book *Mere Christianity*, Lewis details the liar, lunatic, or Lord argument.

> "I am trying here to prevent anyone saying the really foolish thing that people often say about Him: I'm ready to accept Jesus as a great moral teacher, but I don't accept his claim to be God. That is the one thing we must not say. A man who was merely a man and said the sort of things Jesus said would not be a great moral teacher. He would either be a lunatic—on the level with the man who says he is a poached egg—or else he would be the Devil of Hell. You must make your choice. Either this man was, and is, the Son of God, or else a madman or something worse. You can shut him up for a fool, you can spit at him and kill him as a demon or you can fall at his feet and call him Lord and God but let us not come with any patronizing nonsense about his being a great human teacher. He has not left that open to us. He did not intend to. ... Now it seems to me obvious that He was neither a lunatic nor a

44

fiend: and consequently, however strange or
terrifying or unlikely it may seem, I have to
accept the view that He was and is God."[1]

THE ULTIMATE CLAIM

Like Lewis, I believe the evidence shows that Jesus
claimed to be Lord and God. What evidence does the
New Testament give us? We could cite many examples, such as his most often used self-designation as
the Son of Man, his authority to create, forgive,
judge, and accept worship, and his alleged ability to
give eternal life. Here are a few examples that can be
easily explained without a great deal of background
and context.

Are you the Christ?

Shortly before Jesus was taken to Pontius Pilate and
subsequently nailed to the cross, he was taken to the
Jewish high priest, Caiaphas, and questioned. In
Mark 14, he states in the affirmative that he is the
Christ (Messiah), the Son of God. What's more, he
said he will occupy the throne with God and come
riding on the clouds of heaven. We know from the
Old Testament that anyone riding on the clouds is a
reference to God. After hearing Jesus' response,
Caiaphas tore his clothes and declared "blasphemy!"
Both Caiaphas and his fellow Jews knew that Jesus
was not only responding "yes" to his question but
also appealing to a passage in Daniel 7 where the Son
of Man comes on the clouds of heaven with all authority and power over the nations. This Old
Testament passage from Daniel is complimentary to
Mark 14 and included here for reference.

"Again the high priest asked him, 'Are you the Christ, the Son of the Blessed One?' 'I am,' Jesus said. 'And you will see the Son of Man sitting at the right hand of the Mighty One and coming on the clouds of heaven.' The high priest tore his clothes. 'Why do we need any more witnesses?' he asked. 'You have heard the blasphemy. What do you think?' They all condemned him as worthy of death." (Mark 14:61–63)

"In my vision at night I looked, and there before me was one like a son of man, coming with the clouds of heaven. He approached the Ancient of Days and was led into his presence. He was given authority, glory and sovereign power; all peoples, nations, and men of every language worshipped him. His dominion is an everlasting dominion that will not pass away, and his kingdom is one that will never be destroyed." (Daniel 7:13–14)

I am!

The book of John outlines several debates with a Jewish group called the Pharisees while Jesus was in Jerusalem for a feast. During one of these debates, Jesus gave perhaps his most authoritative answer to our question. When Jesus said he had seen Abraham, who died nearly 1,800 years earlier, the Pharisees were perplexed about how that was possible. Jesus then said, "Before Abraham was born, I am!" Their immediate reaction was to stone him. Why? In Exodus 3, Moses encountered God in the burning bush. God instructed Moses to approach the Pharaoh and demand that he release the Israelite people from slavery in Egypt. Knowing that the Israelite people would question his authority and ask who sent him to deliver them from bondage, Moses asked God, "Who should I say sent me?" God responds, "I AM WHO I AM. I AM has sent me to you."

Fast forward to the debate with the Pharisees. These Jewish leaders knew exactly what and who Jesus was referencing. Not only was he saying that he lived before Abraham, but he was also claiming to be the eternal God, Yahweh of the Old Testament. The Pharisees considered this a blasphemous and serious offense, leading to the attempted killing of Jesus. And although it was only an attempted murder during this altercation, Jesus was ultimately killed on the cross for making this statement.

> *"'You are not yet fifty years old,' the Jews said to him, 'and you have seen Abraham!' 'I tell you the truth,' Jesus answered, 'before Abraham was born, I am!' At this, they picked up stones to stone him, but Jesus hid himself, slipping away from the temple grounds."* (John 8:57–59)

> *"Moses said to God, 'Suppose I go to the Israelites and say to them, 'The God of your fathers has sent me to you,' and they ask me, 'What is his name?' Then what shall I tell them?' God said to Moses, 'I AM WHO I AM. This is what you are to say to the Israelites: 'I AM has sent me to you.'"* (Exodus 3:13–14)

Authority to Forgive Sins

As Jesus' ministry spread, more people began to hear about his authoritative teachings and his ability to heal the sick. As the crowds grew, it became more difficult for people to approach Jesus face-to-face, leading to some creative thinking. In a passage in Mark, a group of men brought their paralyzed friend to the house where Jesus was staying. Because the house was full and people were standing outside trying to get a glimpse of Jesus through the windows, they had no way to get their companion to Jesus. Determined to reach him, they decided to climb to the top of the house, dig through the roof, and lower the man down. Upon seeing the faith of this group of men, Jesus said to the paralytic, "Son, your sins are forgiven." To the onlooking Jewish leaders, someone claiming to have the ability to forgive sins meant he was claiming to be God.

> *"Since they could not get him to Jesus because of the crowd, they made an opening in the roof above Jesus and, after digging through it, lowered the mat the paralyzed man was lying on. When Jesus saw their faith, he said to the paralytic, 'Son, your sins are forgiven.' Now some teachers of the law were sitting there, thinking to themselves, 'Why does this fellow talk like that? He's blaspheming! Who can forgive sins but God alone?' Immediately Jesus knew in his spirit that this was what they were thinking in their hearts, and he said to them, 'Why are you thinking these things? Which is easier: to say to the paralytic, "Your sins are forgiven," or to say, "Get up, take your mat and walk"? But that you may know that the Son of Man has authority on earth to forgive sins ...' He said to the paralytic, 'I tell you, get up, take your mat and go home.' He got up, took his mat and walked out in full view of them all."* (Mark 2:4–12)

The information found in these passages appears to provide reasonable evidence that Jesus claimed to be God. The reaction of the Jewish leaders alone confirms this fact. If Jesus was just a good and moral teacher, why would they want to kill him? Apologist Josh McDowell came to a similar conclusion in his book *More Than a Carpenter*. He writes, "Why don't the names of the Buddha, Muhammad, or Confucius offend people the way the name of Jesus does? I think the reason is that these other religious leaders didn't claim to be God."[2]

THE RESURRECTION

In 1 Corinthians 15:14–15, the Apostle Paul says, "And if Christ has not been raised, our preaching is useless and so is your faith. More than that, we are then found to be false witnesses about God, for we have testified about God that he raised Christ from the dead." The resurrection is at the heart of the gospel message; thus, without it, there would be no Christianity. For the skeptic, proving the resurrection as false would be a home run, or better yet, the grand slam of the ages. Yet we have one of the strongest and most reasonable arguments for Christianity specifically within the resurrection.

Due to the immense weight of the resurrection in Christianity, skeptics and believers have debated this topic for decades. One of the most well-known apologists in this field is Dr. Gary Habermas. In the words of Michael Martin, Boston University professor and atheist, "Perhaps the most sophisticated defense of the resurrection to date has been produced by Gary Habermas."[3] Habermas obtained his doctorate from Michigan State University and wrote his dissertation on the resurrection. Since then, he has authored or co-authored more than forty books, about half of them in defense of the resurrection.

What's unique about Habermas' defense of the resurrection is his approach. Although he himself believes the entirety of the Bible as I do, he defends the resurrection by using only material highly agreed on by New Testament scholars, skeptics and believers alike. Highly-agreed upon material, according to Habermas, must have a consensus of ninety-five percent of scholarship. Habermas calls this the "minimal facts" approach. In his own words, he says, "This approach considers only those data that are so strongly attested historically that they are granted by nearly every scholar who studies the subject, even the rather skeptical ones."[4] This unique approach to the defense of the resurrection is compelling to many, particularly the most skeptical. Let's examine this line of reasoning.

It's important to recognize that even extreme skeptics use the Bible to make their point and secure their argument against various Biblical stances. They may not agree that the Bible is inspired by God, but there is enough evidence for certain passages or books of the Bible that skeptics consider them to be authentic texts. So, what books of the Bible are considered "reliable" or "authentic?" Of the thirteen letters attributed to the Apostle Paul, even the most skeptical scholars consider seven of these books the authentic writings by Paul himself. These seven books are Galatians, Philippians, Romans, Philemon, 1 Thessalonians, and 1 and 2 Corinthians. Why do highly skeptical scholars allow these specific books to be used? Paul was an intelligent scholar who studied under the well-known Gamaliel in the first century, was politically aware of what was going on at that time, knew other eyewitnesses to Jesus, and became a convert to Christianity after he had imprisoned Christians in an effort to stifle the very message he later proclaimed. Although seven books can be used and accepted by the skeptic community, a passage in 1 Corinthians will serve as a building block in our defense of the resurrection.

Paul is writing to the church in Corinth as a follow-up to his previous visit. The theme of the letter is that I (Paul) came and preached the message of the gospel to you, and here's a reminder of what I told you. What did you do with that information? 1 Corinthians 15:3–8 says, "For what I received I passed on to you as of first importance: that Christ died for our sins according to the Scriptures, that he was buried, that he was raised on the third day according to the Scriptures, and that he appeared to Peter, and then to the Twelve. After that, he appeared to more than five hundred of the brothers at the same time, most of whom are still living, though some have fallen asleep. Then he appeared to James, then to all the apostles, and last of all he appeared to me also, as to one abnormally born." These six verses have been pointed out by scholars on both sides of the aisle as an early creed, sometimes called an oral tradition or confession.[5] Although just over forty creeds are found throughout the Bible, this one in 1 Corinthians 15 is the most well-known, earliest, and potentially the most significant.

Why are creeds important to the defense of the resurrection and the New Testament in general? In his highly influential book *The Earliest Christian Confessions*, Frenchman Dr. Oscar Cullmann says,

"The need for apostolic summary (creeds) was all the greater, since Christian doctrine existed in oral form only."[6] History tells us that around 90 percent of people living at this time did not know how to read or write, so having a short saying, or as Habermas says, a "ditty" or "poem," was paramount to the message because it could be memorized and thus increase its ability to travel from town to town. This stands to reason. If you didn't have technology or the ability to read or write, how would you pass along important information?

This particular creed is important because of when it was created. Scholars in this field often say that the earliest Christology (study of Christ) is the highest Christology, so determining if this creed was established soon after the death and resurrection of Jesus would impact the reliability of this passage. How early was this creed formed after the cross? Well, according to New Testament scholar Dr. Richard Bauckham, who has been described as one of the most authoritative voices on the New Testament in the world, says, "It's a consensus among scholarship that Paul received this material about AD 35,"[7] which is about two to five years after the cross. Skeptic Robert Funk, the founder of the liberal and controversial Jesus Seminar, agrees that this creed is only two to three years after the cross.[8] This is incredibly significant in the world of ancient literature, where writings about Plutarch, Arrian, and Alexander the Great are accepted as historical fact but were written 400, 425, and 300 years after their deaths.

Let's examine further. Scholars believe that Paul encountered Jesus, or at least he thought he encountered Jesus, on the road to Damascus approximately two years after the resurrection. From there, we see in Galatians 1:16–18 (also considered an authentic book) that after Paul saw Jesus, he traveled to Arabia and was there for three years. Following his time in Arabia, he visited Peter and Jesus' brother, James, in Jerusalem and stayed with them for fifteen days. In the original Greek text for verse 18, Paul uses the word *historesai* to describe the reason for his trip to Jerusalem. This word implies that Paul went to research and investigate the eyewitnesses who said they had seen the risen Jesus. Essentially, he wanted to make sure everyone was on the same page with what had been revealed to him. Later in Galatians 2:6, Paul says of his investigation with these eyewitnesses, "Those men added nothing to my message." So, if Peter and James gave the same gospel message to Paul, they would have had it before Paul. If Paul saw Jesus on the road to Damascus two years after the resurrection and spent fifteen days with Peter and James following his three-year stay in Arabia, this is no later than five years after the cross. Scholars then provide additional evidence demonstrating how long a creed takes to form and how widespread this knowledge already was by the time Peter, James, and Paul compared notes. In the words of Gerd Lüdemann, atheist New Testament professor at Göttingen, "… the elements in the tradition are to be dated to the first two years after the crucifixion of Jesus … not later than three years … the formation of the appearance traditions mentioned in 1 Corinthians 15:3–8 falls into the time between 30 and 33 CE."[9] To have this level of detail for a specific event in ancient history is unparalleled.

Now that we have established that this information was being codified and communicated soon after the crucifixion, it's important to discuss the appearances mentioned in verses five through eight. What's the best explanation for these appearances? Was this group of people simply hallucinating due to the immense grief of losing their fearless leader? According to atheist Bart D. Ehrman, Jesus' followers truly *believed* they had seen the risen Christ. "It is a historical fact that some of Jesus' followers came to believe that he had been raised from the dead soon after his execution," Ehrman writes. "We know some of these believers by name; one of them, the apostle Paul, claims quite plainly to have seen Jesus alive after his death. Thus, for the historian, Christianity begins after the death of Jesus, not with the resurrection itself, but with the belief in the resurrection."[10] Although Ehrman believes the disciples truly believed they saw Jesus alive, he does not actually believe they encountered him and, as a result, does not believe in the resurrection himself. He believes the followers either had similar visions or a group hallucination. But in verse six, Paul says something important about Jesus' appearance to the 500 brothers. In a matter-of-fact way, Paul says that most of these people "are still living." Why did he include that statement? Paul was literally *inviting* the readers to fact-check his claims by finding witnesses who saw Jesus after his resurrection and investigating for themselves. If you were planning to spread a lie, would you encourage all hearers to verify what you've said with other eyewitnesses to the event? And as rare as hallucinations are, is it reasonable to think that 500 hundred people had a matching hallucination? Clinical psychologist Dr. Gary L. Collins says the following about group hallucinations: "Hallucinations are individual occurrences. By their very nature, only one person can see a given hallucination at one time. They certainly aren't something which can be seen by a group of people. Neither is it possible that one person could somehow induce a hallucination in somebody else. Since a hallucination exists only in this subjective, personal sense, it is obvious that others cannot witness it."[11] Have you ever been a part of a group hallucination?

So, if the hallucination theory can't account for the resurrection appearances, maybe Jesus never actually died on the cross? Maybe the disciples *did* encounter Jesus, but there was no bodily resurrection because there was no actual death. When one digs further, this theory appears to have some issues. First, the Romans had perfected this method of execution. The significant flogging and subsequent nailing to the cross has been examined by medical experts over the years. In a 1986 issue of the *Journal of the American Medical Association* (JAMA), a group of experts provided their thoughts on the crucifixion. "The usual instrument was a short whip ... with several single or braided leather thongs of variable lengths, in which small iron balls or sharp pieces of sheep bones were tied at intervals ... the man was stripped of his clothing and his hands were tied to an upright post ... The back, buttocks, and legs were flogged. ... The scourging ... was intended to weaken the victim to a state just short of collapse or death. ... As the Roman soldiers repeatedly struck the victim's back with full force, the iron balls would cause deep contusions and the leather thongs and sheep bones would cut into the skin and subcutaneous tissues. Then, as the flogging continued, the lacerations would tear into the underlying skeletal muscles."[12]

Furthermore, as referenced in the previous section, Roman soldiers would often stab the side of the individual on the cross to confirm his death. In John

19:34, it says, "One of the soldiers pierced his side with a spear, and immediately there came out blood and water." This mixture of blood and water is caused by a buildup of fluid near the heart from an intense beating. Again, we now know this to be called pericardial effusion. Finally, if Jesus did not actually die on the cross but rather regained consciousness and reappeared, would the disciples believe this man with a mutilated body was God and worthy of following? Seeing Jesus in this state would have undoubtedly caused the disciples to turn away from Him, a far cry from the boldness unto death we examined earlier.

Although there are several alternative theories one should explore for post-resurrection appearances, I agree with Habermas' words: "Sometimes people just grasp at straws trying to account for the appearances. But nothing fits the evidence better than the explanation that Jesus was alive."[13]

CONCLUSION

The focus of this chapter was on Jesus. Was he who he claimed to be, and did he rise from the grave? After a rational discussion contemplating whether he was a liar, a lunatic, or Lord, reasonable evidence indicates that he indeed claimed to be God. From there, we investigated a passage from 1 Corinthians to build the case for his resurrection following his death on the cross.

Now, I will grant you that someone dying and rising from the dead three days later is difficult to comprehend. And for you, maybe it's the biggest roadblock of all. On the surface, it seems irrational and unreasonable. But, if there is a God and the Bible is a reliable document, is it all that unreasonable? I believe the evidence suggests that the alternative theories of his resurrection have serious complications and that the written accounts and early creeds prove his resurrection beyond a reasonable doubt.

THE FINAL VERDICT

At the start of this book, I stated that our goal was to answer three broad questions beyond a reasonable doubt. A chapter was devoted to each question, and ultimately worked together to build the case for a final verdict on truth.

The first chapter provided evidence for a personal God who created the universe from nothing, precisely orchestrated its arrangement to an unfathomable exactness, designed biological life with extraordinary detail and order, and wrote a transcendent standard of rightness on the hearts and minds of every human being.

The second chapter provided evidence for the historical reliability of the Bible. We examined non-Christian writings, archaeology, eyewitness accounts, the martyrdom of the disciples, the sheer volume of manuscripts, the accuracy of those manuscripts, and fulfilled prophecies to build our case.

The third chapter provided evidence for Jesus' claims to be God and his resurrection from the dead. Through deduction, we saw evidence for Jesus being neither a liar nor a lunatic but Lord and God. We investigated not only the resurrection itself, but also potential alternative theories to the apparent sightings of Jesus after his death on the cross.

Now we've come to a decision point. The evidence has been presented, and you are the sole jury member. The outcome of this trial isn't deciding whether or not you pay for a traffic violation. It's determining the trajectory of your life and where you'll spend eternity. You see, if God is real, the Bible is true, and Jesus died on the cross and rose from the dead, it's the greatest story ever told. It means that God sent his perfect son, Jesus, to die on the cross for the sins of this world. What sins, you may ask? You might be thinking, I've done a few bad things, but overall, I'm a good person. Surely, if there's a God, I'll still go to heaven. If I bought you a fifty-foot TV, placed it in the middle of Times Square, and began playing a movie of your life, what would people see? It's a sobering thought, isn't it? It certainly is for me.

The Bible says the wages or payment of that sin is eternity apart from God. Why? Because of the seriousness of sin and the holiness of God. But by his grace, Jesus paid our debt through his death on the cross. And you know what? If you were the only person on earth, Jesus would have died for *you*. He loves you, he cares for you, and his desire is for you to spend eternity with him.

No one can tell you what to do. The judge's gavel is raised and ready. What's your verdict?

IGNORING THE PROOF?

The title of this book is *Proof You Can't Ignore*. Throughout the book, I've introduced many pieces of evidence—evidence that I believe is reasonably documented and substantiated beyond a reasonable doubt. Much like a court case, when someone is presented with this amount of evidence, they can choose to accept or reject it, but it cannot be ignored outright. You must do *something* with it. Now, you can certainly reject the evidence based on your evaluation. You're entitled to that position in just the same way I am entitled to accept it. Conversely, many reject God, Jesus, and the Bible not because of the lack of evidence, but for another reason. Namely, if this so-called God is a just and good God, why is there evil in this world? Why does God allow bad things to happen?

When this question is posed, my immediate instinct is to attempt to provide the most logical explanation. At a high-level view, this typically involves a response stating that God created us with free will. We aren't robots programmed to love God. If he wanted robots, he would have created robots. But he wanted to create a being that had a choice, a choice to *choose* to love him and be in a relationship with him. And if God created us with free will, it necessarily opens the possibility of evil. Said in another way, if you ask God to stop evil, you are ultimately asking him to take away your freedom as a human being to make decisions. God can't create people with free will and require that they follow him; it's a logical contradiction. But as I alluded to earlier, my immediate response, quite often, is not the appropriate response.

This type of answer does little for the person who has truly suffered heartache. For the father who has lost a young child, for the wife in an abusive relationship, for the little boy who endured years of heartless parents, for the man who lives every day with a debilitating disease, this is not an adequate answer. The truth is, I do not know why God allows these things to happen. I cannot begin to imagine some of the things that many of you have gone through in this life, let alone attempt to explain them. But I humbly believe that there is hope in this world despite it all. And if you think I am suggesting, at this point, that becoming a Christian nullifies any future hardships, I can assure you this is not the case. (One only needs to read the book of Job in the Old Testament to grasp a sense of the difficulties that a believer can face.) True believers *expect* difficulty, but they have both hope and a companion. The Bible says Jesus is a friend who sticks closer than a brother. And let me tell you, my friend, Jesus is as close as a prayer.

You can decide to turn your life over to Him by turning from sin, believing that He died on the cross for your sins and that He rose from the dead to save you and to save me. And, speaking from experience, you will not be the same if you make that decision.

The Bible says, "Anyone who belongs to Christ has become a new person. The old life is gone; a new life has begun!" (2 Cor. 5:17) Admittedly, much of my life I have been passive in sharing this with other people. I was concerned about what people might think or if they would be offended by what I had to say. But over time, I realized that if this is indeed true, the most compassionate thing I could do is tell others what the evidence has told me. As my old friend Dale says, "I'm just one beggar trying to tell another beggar where to find bread."

RESOURCES FOR FURTHER EVIDENCE

Blomberg, Craig – *The Historical Reliability of the New Testament*

Geisler, Norm, and Turek, Frank – *I Don't Have Enough Faith to Be An Atheist*

Habermas, Gary – *The Historical Jesus: Ancient Evidence for the Life of Christ*

Habermas, Gary, and Licona, Michael – *The Case for the Resurrection of Jesus*

Kennedy, Titus – *Unearthing the Bible: 101 Archaeological Discoveries That Bring the Bible to Life*

Lennox, John – *Can Science Explain Everything?*

Lennox, John – *Seven Days That Divide the World: The Beginning According to Genesis and Science*

Lewis, C.S. – *Mere Christianity*

McDowell, Josh – *Evidence That Demands a Verdict*

McFarland, Alex – *The 10 Most Common Objections to Christianity*

McFarland, Alex and Harper, Bert – *100 Bible Questions and Answers*

Metaxas, Eric – *Is Atheism Dead?*

Meyer, Stephen – *Signature in the Cell: DNA and the Evidence for Intelligent Design*

Meyer, Stephen – *Darwin's Doubt: The Explosive Origin of Animal Life and the Case for Intelligent Design*
Ross, Hugh – *Designed to the Core*
Ross, Hugh – *Why the Universe Is the Way It Is*
Strobel, Lee – *The Case for Christ: A Journalist's Personal Investigation of the Evidence for Jesus*
Wallace, J. Warner – *Cold-Case Christianity: A Homicide Detective Investigates the Claims of the Gospels*

NOTES

Chapter 1

1. Lee Strobel (@LeeStrobel), Twitter (now X), December 24, 2017, https://x.com/LeeStrobel/status/944981555587506176.

2. Norman L. Geisler and Frank Turek, *I Don't Have Enough Faith to Be an Atheist* (Wheaton, IL: Crossway, 2004), 76–78.

3. Geisler and Turek, *I Don't Have Enough Faith to Be an Atheist,* 79–81.

4. Geisler and Turek, *I Don't Have Enough Faith to Be an Atheist,* 81–82.

5. Geisler and Turek, *I Don't Have Enough Faith to Be an Atheist,* 82–83.

6. Geisler and Turek, *I Don't Have Enough Faith to Be an Atheist,* 83–84.

7. Hugh Ross PhD, *The Creator and the Cosmos: How the Greatest Scientific Discoveries of the Century Reveal God* (Third Expanded Edition) (Colorado Springs: NavPress, 2001), 56.

8. Eric Metaxas, *Is Atheism Dead?* (Washington, D.C.: Salem Books, 2021), 35.

9. Richard Dawkins, "Fine-Tuning is a Good Argument for God," on The Big Conversation. Posted May 29, 2022, by Premier Unbelievable?, YouTube, https://youtu.be/apWOkC7krfQ?si=Z1JbW0a7Xhfdzhe4.

10. Metaxas, *Is Atheism Dead?,* 42.

11. Hugh Ross, *Why the Universe Is the Way It Is* (Grand Rapids, Michigan: Baker Books, 2008), 65–67.

12. Metaxas, *Is Atheism Dead?,* 63.

13. Geisler and Turek, *I Don't Have Enough Faith to Be an Atheist,* 98.

14. Geisler and Turek, *I Don't Have Enough Faith to Be an Atheist,* 101.

15. Geisler and Turek, *I Don't Have Enough Faith to Be an Atheist,* 102.

16. Ross, *Why the Universe Is the Way It Is,* 83.

17. Ross, *Why the Universe Is the Way It Is,* 80.

18. Metaxas, *Is Atheism Dead?*, 56.

19. Metaxas, *Is Atheism Dead?*, 66–67.

20. Metaxas, *Is Atheism Dead?*, 58.

21. John C. Lennox, *Can Science Explain Everything?* (India: The Good Book Company, 2024), 50.

22. John C. Lennox, *Can Science Explain Everything?*, 41–42.

23. Richard Dawkins, *The Blind Watchmaker* (New York: Norton, 1987), 116.

24. Stephen C. Meyer, *Signature in the Cell: DNA and the Evidence for Intelligent Design* (San Francisco: HarperOne, 2009), 212.

25. Geisler and Turek, *I Don't Have Enough Faith to Be an Atheist* (Wheaton, IL: Crossway, 2004), 176.

Chapter 2

1. *The Bible: The Believers Gain, Time*, December 30, 1974, https://time.com/archive/6842866/the-biblethe-believers-gain/.

2. Alex McFarland and Bert Harper, *100 Bible Questions and Answers: Inspiring Truths, Historical Facts, Practical Insights*, (Savage, MN: BroadStreet Publishing, 2021), 14.

3. Josh McDowell and Sean McDowell, *Evidence for Jesus* (Nashville, TN: Thomas Nelson, 2023), 12.

4. Alexander Roberts and James Donaldson, eds. *Ante-Nicene Christian Library: Translations of the Writings of the Fathers Down to A.D. 325*, vol. 9, *Iraneus, Vol. II-Hippolytus, Vol. II-Fragments of Third Century* (Edinburgh: T & T Clark, 1870), 188.

5. Roberts and Donaldson, eds. *Ante-Nicene Christian Library*, 188.

6. Josh McDowell, *The New Evidence That Demands a Verdict* (San Bernadino, California. Here's to Life Publishers, 1981), 55.

7. Shlomo Pines, *An Arabic Version of the Testimonium Flavianum and Its* Implications (Israel Academy of Sciences and Humanities: Jerusalem, 1971), Kindle edition, Kindle locations 9-10, 16.

8. McDowell, *The New Evidence That Demands a Verdict*, 55-57.

9. Titus Kennedy, *Unearthing the Bible: 101 Archaeological Discoveries that bring the Bible to life*

(Eugene, Oregon: Harvest House Publishers, 2020), 190.

10. Kennedy, *Unearthing the Bible: 101 Archaeological Discoveries that bring the Bible to life*, 190–191.

11. Kennedy, *Unearthing the Bible: 101 Archaeological Discoveries that bring the Bible to life* 98–99.

12. Kennedy, *Unearthing the Bible: 101 Archaeological Discoveries that bring the Bible to life*, 188–189.

13. Kennedy, *Unearthing the Bible: 101 Archaeological Discoveries that bring the Bible to life*, 48–49.

14. Metaxas, *Is Atheism Dead?*, 151–159.

15. Geisler and Turek, *I Don't Have Enough Faith to Be an Atheist*, 225.

16. Craig L. Blomberg, *The Historical Reliability of the New Testament* (Brentwood, Tennessee: B&H Academic, 2016), 613.

17. Geisler and Turek, *I Don't Have Enough Faith to Be an Atheist*, 225.

18. Geisler and Turek, *I Don't Have Enough Faith to Be an Atheist*, 227.

19. Josh McDowell, *Evidence That Demands a Verdict: Historical Evidences for the Christian Faith* (Nashville, TN: Thomas Nelson, Inc., 1979), 48.

20. Archeaology Helps to Confirm the Historicity of the Bible – Josh.org/ Josh.org. Published January 31, 2018. https://www.josh.org/archeology-validates-bible/.

21. Craig L. Blomberg, *The Historical Reliability of the New Testament*, (Brentwood, Tennessee: B&H Academic, 2016), 612.

22. Blomberg, *The Historical Reliability of the New Testament*, 614.

23. Blomberg, *The Historical Reliability of the New Testament*, 614.

24. Blomberg, *The Historical Reliability of the New Testament*

25. Blomberg, *The Historical Reliability of the New Testament*, 645.

26. J. Warner Wallace, *Cold-Case Christianity: A Homicide Detective Investigates the Claims of the Gospels* (Colorado Springs, CO: David C Cook, 2013), 162–163.

27. Geisler and Turek, *I Don't Have Enough Faith to Be an Atheist*, 235–243.

28. Wallace, *Cold-Case Christianity: A Homicide Detective Investigates the Claims of the Gospels*, 86.

Chapter 3

1. C.S. Lewis, *Mere Christianity (New York, NY: HarperCollins, 1972)*, 55-56.

2. Josh McDowell, *More Than a Carpenter* (Carol Stream, IL: Tyndale House Publishers, 2024), 9.

3. Lee Strobel, *The Case for Easter, A Journalist Investigates Evidence for the Resurrection* (Grand Rapids, MI: Zondervan, 2003), 60.

4. Habermas and Licona, *The Case for the Resurrection of Jesus*, (Grand Rapids, MI: Kregel Inc., 2004) 44.

5. Habermas and Licona, *The Case for the Resurrection of Jesus* 52-53.

6. Oscar Cullman, translated by J.K. S Reid, *The Earliest Christian Confessions* (Eugene, OR: Wipf and Stock Publishers, 2018) 10.

7. Habermas, Gary, "The Resurrection Argument that Changed a Generation of Scholars," Posted 2013, by The Veritas Forum, YouTube, https://www.youtube.com/watch?v=ay_Db4R wZ_M

8. Roy W. Hoover, *The Acts of Jesus* (Santa Rosa, CA: Polebridge Press, 1998), 466.

9. Gerd Lüdemann, *The Resurrection of Jesus: History, Experience, Theology* (Minneapolis, MN: Fortress, 1994), 171-72.

10. Bart Ehrman, *The New Testament: A Historical Introduction to the Early Christian Writings*, (Third Edition New York, Oxford: Oxford University Press, 2004), 276.

11. Strobel, *The Case for Easter, A Journalist Investigates Evidence for the Resurrection*, 79.

12. Habermas and Licona, *The Case for the Resurrection of Jesus*, 100.

13. Strobel, *The Case for Easter, A Journalist Investigates Evidence for the Resurrection*, 81.